The Afterlife of Trees

The Hugh MacLennan Poetry Series

Editors: Kerry McSweeney and Joan Harcourt
Selection Committee: Donald H. Akenson,
Philip Cercone, Jane Everett,
and Carolyn Smart

TITLES IN THE SERIES

THE
AFTERLIFE
OF TREES

Brian Bartlett

McGill-Queen's University Press
Montreal & Kingston · London · Ithaca

© McGill-Queen's University Press 2002
ISBN 0-7735-1910-6

Legal deposit first quarter 2002
Bibliothèque nationale du Québec

Printed in Canada on acid-free paper

McGill-Queen's University Press acknowledges the
financial support of the Government of Canada through
the Book Publishing Industry Development Program
(BPIDP) for its publishing activities. We also
acknowledge the support of the Canada Council
for the Arts for our publishing program.

**National Library of Canada Cataloguing
in Publication Data**

Bartlett, Brian, 1953–
The afterlife of trees
(The Hugh MacLennan poetry series)
Poems.
ISBN 0-7735-1910-6
I. Title. II. Series: Hugh MacLennan poetry series.
PS8553.A773A74 2002   C811'.54   C2001-903320-6
PR9199.3.B374A74 2002

This book was typeset by Dynagram Inc.
in 9.5/13 New Baskerville.

for

Joshua and Laura

in their beginnings

CONTENTS

The German words *Buch* (book), *Buche* (beech), *Buchsbaum* (boxwood), the English words book, bush, etc., and the French words *bois* (wood), *bosquet* (little wood), *buis* (boxtree), *bûche* (log), and *bouquin* (slang for book) all have the same root and are derived from *boscus* (wood in Latin). In Irish and Gaelic the same word designated tree and letter ...

... Writing has become today the main consumer of wood, the essential outlet of forests, the abyss in which the press each day sends entire forests.

– Roland Bechmann, *Trees and Man:*
The Forest in the Middle Ages,
trans. Katharyn Dunham

A BOX FOR SMALL BIRTHS

LISTENING ON THE BACK STEPS

You're glad when one word from your keyboard
startles you. Some days even more than that
takes flight, then you stand back
                              to see what you've made:
a box for small births, wings fluttering
under the roof. So you've managed to offer
some grubs, and a home of waterproof wood.

But whenever you read those whose words
surround you like a new kind of weather,
you see who you are:

you're the one who climbs out the window
                              while his parents sleep
and walks many blocks to where the music is played –
the Panama, Greenleaf Gardens, the Novelty Club.
Too young to get in, you haunt the back steps
craning toward a door propped open with a brick
until your ears hum and burn. Your heart quickens
when you hear a sound rise above the others,
                              its slow fat notes,
                                   fast agile ones,
the shocks of unexpected accents.

Home with your sax, hungry to learn, you practice
at dawn, noon, dusk. Years pass like hastily scanned

bars of notes. No matter how much you make
some corner of your neighbourhood sing,
you know you'll never leave those steps –

short-breathed, hunched, listening to that voice
burst through the doorway and float through the night
and swing open whatever is shut, whatever needs more air.

4

HOW ACUPUNCTURE IS LIKE POETRY

The end of my tongue tingles from the needle in my chest.

LOST FOOTNOTE
FROM AN ESSAY ON RHYTHM

after watching four Buster Keaton movies in one weekend

Walking dulls a pinch in the shoulders, sharpens a thought
      in the mind – tells me the measure is right,
the machine running smooth. On days rare as lightning, a different urge

      pulls me up like wind from the back:
I would run with lungs of limitless air, speed
      down streets with no time to read their names,

spring over walls and shrubs with breath-giving grace.
      While I walk, light-sneakered, I watch another
break from my blood and run:

      finding the cheetah or Keaton within, he stops traffic
as if danger didn't exist, leaps through an open window
      and out an open door, splashes through a stream

like a stallion unstrapped from its harness, inhales
      and exhales up a hill and down,
starts a rockslide that sends boulders bounding past

      his shoulders. He doesn't care if anyone –
a gang of cops or howling children, the hound of heaven –
      chases him. Neither escape nor search,

6

the race is all muscle thrill and blood surge,
>going back to the day a Cro-Magnon first
laughed because he could run for no reason.

>When he's dashed, swerved, and flown for hours,
a raindrop-simple thought falls:
>>*in a place I can hardly recall, a deep chair*

waits with a footstool and a full glass.
>But for a minute more he knows
fence-leaping freedom, heart-charging nimbleness,

a spring gushing, unstoppable, along the earth –

SHUFFLES

for Rosemary and Ricky Talbot

winter blooms, turns
and throws across snow
shadows, light, leaves, a child

        winter leaves turn and
        a child blooms, throws
        snow light across shadows

across light blooms and leaves
winter throws turns,
snow shadows a child

        snow light throws blooms
        across winter: a shadow child
        turns and leaves

        *

hear the story leap
and the breath whisper
and roar through you

        story the breath
        and hear you roar
        and leap through the whisper

breath through story:
you roar the whisper and
hear the leap and –

                                you hear, whisper and leap
                                and roar the breath
                                through the story

TWO FOR THE WINDS

1

The forest was still, like a lake where no reed wavers.

Light filtered through, but didn't pick at the needles.

Tall ferns bowed under their own weight.

Only crouching to ants aswarm on their hill
would've brought you any drama
worth inviting a crowd to.

One dangling strip of birchbark
                                    started to shake.

That seemed a beginning, a door opening –

but the one strip went on shaking
and nothing else stirred.

The breeze that flowed against the bark
was an ongoing puff,

isolated as a slip-trickle in a desert,

minor
yet major
because it moved the one thing that moved.

2

These winds that lift our garbage lids would
                              lift our scalps
if they could! Twigs spin down the air, a flag
jumbles a province's symbols. Plastic bags tangled high
                              in bare trees, whipped, turn
inside-out, rightside-out, inside-
out. What meeting of airs stirred up such motion
and commotion? No wonder our ancestors
pictured satchels the size of mountains,
gods with bursting cheeks. These are the winds
that break the reins of everything tamed.
A roof tile torn from its nails slices the air,
spins and falls. Blinking, a baby's eyes water
and the mother pushing the stroller stops,
spreads her arms across the opening. Turret
by turret, a castle in a sandbox slides apart;
a tennis court looks abandoned forever. These winds
refuse to point out

        "which way the wind blows." In the harbour, waves
shoot flat across a sailboat's bow, and the ferry
needs twice its usual time to cross
with no one on the top deck but a man reading,
holding the pages down, his face embattled.

All day, light rubbed and streamed over everything on shore
    but other than noting
overriding blue, I hardly gave the sky a thought.
    Far past midnight
when I slid from sleep and out of the tent,
    the star-jammed
blackness nearly threw me on my back. Then the sky
    was the one thing
to watch, like a billion acres of voices and signals
    demanding attention,
more than any shivering man could do. Had I ever been
    so awake? –
yet I couldn't answer *hey you, you, you, you, you*
    all at once. My eyes
filled up with brightnesses flung from farther
    than I'll ever go.

I recalled an Italian count, some novel's sullen brooder,
    dubbing the sky
"old roof," saying our sins had plastered it with centuries
    of gloom,
and I knew all kinds of our junk ripped and zipped past
    out there.
Still, imprinted with the day, I searched for constellations
    never named –
Seal, Tern, Heron, Sandpiper – and felt the sky was some
    limitless mind
dancing, or a sea of secrets suddenly breaking through.

Under the taken-for-granted blue,
the first seal surfacing
had seemed a stranger wading ashore
after days hugging flotsam,
forehead masked in black hair.

Glistening amidst
many glistenings, sleekness
complete, two others
lifted their heads, bobbed and
stared, stared and bobbed –
"like beings off a U.F.O."
I thought at the tide's edge
but they could've barked
 What's your business, alien
 glaring at us? What world of little hair
 have you travelled from?

Above the driftwood line, a toad
sluggishly hopped
across leafy mulch, then
went still, so intent on camouflage
I felt a pinprick of guilt
just watching, scribbling
mental notes on his ridges and lumps.
When he inched under
greater safety, my boot nudged

aside the bleached board,
robbing him of cover.

He raised no frightened eyes
to me, who might've been
a tall monstrosity to him
(or merely useless
like a bathing suit to a seal,
a flashlight to the stars).

*

Where 3 a.m. blackness swallowed the beach,
I couldn't find one new constellation
among the neck-spraining masses of stars.

Back in the tent, the day's creatures
gathered around the balled-up jacket of my pillow.
A double darkness of night and tent
encased me,
              yet dragonfly and blood worm and heron
darted, burrowed, and stalked in the sides
of my side vision, each a tangle of urges and cells.
On the edge of sleep
three pairs of eyes glistened among waves.

THE COLOURS AT MCCORMACK'S BEACH

High tide turning, thin light tracks the rocks,
all their greys and whites. Overtaken by fog
Lawlor Island is lost out there
and we must be lost to it
while warning drones rumble,
the bass in the morning's spare music.
Around the horseshoe-shaped boardwalk
a poodle fights restraint, yet makes
no sound. A man at the other end of the leash
scolds; the dog's name sounds like "Wooster!"

One willet feeds at the shoreline. Nothing
else veers into sight. No fin surfaces,
no boat slides past. Dullness on everything – except
stretches of brittle grasses, where flowers
ignite, a slow burn in the damp: hawkweed, goldenrod,
wild mustard, evening primroses, butter-and-eggs,
swamp candles – from lemon to layered yellow
to dark gold and back.

Too much themselves to need the sun
as prototype, they're sopranos to our sight,
feeding off the slightest, most staggered
slivers of light. We wouldn't need
much more to believe yellow specks,
blown afield, dust with microscopic dust
the willet's wings, the dog's paws, the man's beard.

SLOTH SURPRISES

Like a rainbow before breakfast, a sloth is a surprise,
an unexpected fellow breather of the air of our planet.
No one could prophesy a sloth.

        – William Beebe, *Jungle Days**

How would you feel hanging in cecropia trees
   until algae slicks your fur? Would you flinch
at being called a termite nest, a doormat draped

   around a branch, the mop-head butt of naturalist jokes?
("a masterpiece of immobility ..." "an enthusiasm for life
   excelled by a healthy sunflower ...

the second hand of a watch often covers
   more distance"). And what flips and flops
would your ego do if you were named in honour

   of a Deadly Sin? Its Spanish nickname:
Perico Ligero (Nimble Peter), better praise than *Sloth*.
   Lethargy and listlessness are all

many think of it, lazily. Even a sloth Website
   (yes, there are a few) kicks off with comedy:
the William Tell Overture galloping

* other quotations in the poem are from Lorus and Margery Milne,
 Beebe, and Charles Waterton

from Packard Bell speakers. Pointing out
they sleep eighteen hours a day is like announcing
          dolphins leap, wolves howl, and gulls

tear garbage apart. What I want is what
          shakes up the known. Give me
the sport of snails, the mourning of sparrows,

          the rage of porcupines. I'm still waiting
to hear the worm that sings. Though no giraffe,
          the sloth could boast (if it chose to) the most

neck vertebrae of any mammal, the greatest range
          of temperatures. Caterpillars in its algae-matted coat
become moths that sip water from its nostrils and eyes.

          "Life disputes with death every inch of flesh ...
I saw the heart of one beat for half an hour
          after it was taken out of the body."

And it swims, how it swims! When the Amazon
          rises higher, sloths cross a mile underwater
in no time, swinging their long forelimbs one

          after the other, blending dexterity and force.
Destined for other trees and camouflage,
          their hearts pick up speed, their great claws

cut water spangled with startled fish. All
associations of sin wash from their thick fur.
Sloths swim with the might of eagles flying.

THE AFTERLIFE OF TREES

for Don McKay

Neither sheep nor cows crisscross our lives as much.
Trees dangle apples and nuts for the hungry, throw
shade down for lovers, mark sites for the lost,
and first and last are
utterly themselves,
fuller and finer than any letter or number,
any 7 or T. Their fragmentary afterlife goes on
in a guitar's body and a hockey stick, in the beaked faces
up a totem pole and the stake through a vampire's heart,
in a fragrant cheese-board, a Welsh love-spoon,
a sweat-stained axe handle, a giant green dragonfly
suspended from the ceiling with twine,
in the spellbinding shapechanging
behind a glass woodstove-door …

and in a table I sanded and finished this week.
– *Finished?* – Four grades of sandpaper drew out
alder's "nature," inimitable amoeba shapes,
waves, half-moons, paw prints dissolving in mud.
What looks more beautiful after death? We sand
and sand, but under the stain, beyond our pottery
and books, our fallen hairs trapped in the varnish,
something remains like memories of a buck
rubbing its horns on bark. Soaked in
deeper than the grain goes: cries, whistles, hoots.

A TOSS OF CONES

Twelve months, and one more ring to the tree –
a measurement of years, hidden as our marrow.
Show me a table that grows like that.

No alder chair lets leaves go in October
and unfolds others in May. No birch garden-stake
twists to left or right, thirsty for sunlight.
A bird's-eye-maple bowl doesn't throw
many-branched shadows over the ground
any more than ashes broadcast on the wind
are a man or woman remembered and mourned.

Don't talk to me about the afterlife of trees.
I need places where sap drops in a bucket
and jack pines start up through fire-blackened soil,

where wingseeds spin down through air, a toss
of cones on the orange earth.

In a minute you can walk – for now,
you can walk – from dim woods where firs
squeeze out other firs,

                              to a lone butternut tree on a riverbank
spreading its limbs like an embrace of the air.

After breathing paper too long, be glad to know
a white elm drinks fifteen hundred gallons of water
from a hot dawn to a hot dusk

and Moroccan goats climb to the highest branches
                              of argan trees
to eat the sweet leaves and bark.

A LAKE NAMED AFTER MY ANCESTORS

I haven't seen it in years. Even then the iron tracks
on the overlooking ridge seemed forever silent.
The sun was the only train that warmed the rails.
I would walk between rusted lines, over
split ties, and never hear rumbles or whistles
announcing imminence. Below, a lake not much bigger
than a baseball field, a spattering of white water-lilies
at one end, spruce hemming the water in.

I can't recall otters' backs shining, mergansers
surfacing; no makeshift raft, no oil patch
inched between the shores. Despite the lake's plainness,
with my first camera I caught something of it
and framed an enlargement – a Father's Day present.
I wish I could list splendours of the lake named
after my ancestors – a craggy island, light
tinting the blue water purple, boulders
like stepping stones to an underwater paradise –
but I remember an unpopulated blankness
as if it were awaiting settlement
and meaning, locked in a time when the land
was young as egg and sperm.

I never measured its depths, and have no
stories to tell about it. What did my father think
when he absentmindedly glanced at it
above his pens and envelopes? "If not for my name,
it would be nothing"? On those tracks I was distant
and dry, no more real than the no-see-ums
that must've made shattered haloes over the water,
the breeding, big-throated frogs I'm guessing
were there. Why, just once, didn't I scramble
down the ridge and plunge in?

THE BASEMENT
THAT BECAME A GARDEN

Smokebushes and sedum climb what was once a hearth.
When the house in ruins still held together, a man
crashed through a rotted floor, breaking a knee
to pieces. The owners vowed to tear down
what was left – but the foundation walls
were a misery to move. So with trowels and seeds
they slowly made a sanctuary of blooms.

The dirt floor has given way to grassy loam
brightened by buttercups. Sunlight and rain fall
among the giant stones, feeding whatever's planted
and whatever blows in. A luna-moth caterpillar,
lime green speckled
illuminated-manuscript gold,
feeds on a darker leaf.

Whatever's planted and whatever blows in
flourish. But a woman resting on a stone,
her face shaded by a straw hat beginning
to unravel, thinks:
    Some nights the rocks must recall
when they were below, when spiders wove sticky tendrils

above homemade jams and baskets of potatoes
– and the sky was nothing but a rumour – and mice
multiplied in one corner, born
blind and naked like thoughts at their rawest.
Warmed by the sun, these boulders must crave
those damp tongues of mildew,
that daytime night, the old familiar cold.

GARDENING UNTIL DARK

1   four cats among the flowers

Two are invisible, under the monkshood –
old Zoot who went blind, circling on the spot
as a tumour gnawed his brain, young Hopewell
whose name turned ironic when a taxi
cracked her skull.
                          The other two bash into the lilies,
bushwhack through the hostas. All pizzazz
until the heat drugs them into sleep, they mock
treating gardens like rare glass bowls
dusted once a day with feathers and breath.
Each paw-snapped stem and tail-shattered petal
honours the two swaddled in towels and buried,
their jumps onto the oil tank, their slow-
stepping sureness along the broken fence.

The living snack on beetles and spiders. One
creeps up behind our Rasta neighbour,
gives us a haiku:
                Dreadlocks dangling down
                his back, to his waist. Tempting,
                four paws – spring high!

For trying to pirate the biggest clay pot
but dropping it near the gate, where it smashed:
    your pillows filled with brambles and thorns.

For carrying off the cedar bird-feeder:
    blue-jay shit stuffing your Christmas turkey.

For digging up the azalea bush when it wasn't
in bloom, when you needed to know it
    to want it: a kinked back, muscles on fire.

For stripping the rhubarb patch bare
but for a few tattered leaves:
    bitter dessert curling your tongue.

For cutting the wire we'd hoped would keep
the plastic bird-feeder where it was, but didn't:
    boisterous crows on your roof at 4 a.m.

the yard's more garden than grass and the grass fights
fiercely for its bit of life in the sparse sunlight in the shade
thrown from a neighbouring brick building where lawyers
psychologists and t-shirt designers wrangle deals doctor
minds cook up logos their windows facing the yard where
we've never been leashed to a lawnmower but here i am
with a whippersnipper not just trimming the tricky edges
but the whole lawn the little there is of it whippersnipping
snipperwhipping to keep the height of the grass down to
make its scraggliness look a little shaved thinking why try
to tame what's worked so hard to poke up a few inches at
the sun whose light falls equally upon the frailest green
blade the grandest bloom the baldest patch meanwhile i
have ugly thoughts about the ideal of the perfect lawn and
how it splits green men from ear to ear while the thin
plastic strip which could slice the tail off a mole or shred a
swallowtail sipping at a flower spins with a highpitched
scream whips and snips and steered by my hands powered
by my finger whips whips whips

Descendants of furry stowaways from the harbour,
  gnawers of wires and bricks and cinder blocks,
    figures of mythic dread, well-hidden citizens,
      rats outnumber us down these streets –
    but we rarely meet face to face, so today
  when I stared into those startled eyes
I wished I weren't on my knees. Nose bristling,

it quivered with alertness, as if debating *Leap,*
  or retreat? Seconds later, it vanished
    into our compost heap   – .
      My heart took a minute to regain
    its rhythm. Among dropped peony blossoms
  I wondered if my son's stroller needed a veil,
tooth-proof. But as I rose to my feet

instead of thinking *Typhus, trichinosis,*
  the ship in Nosferatu *aswarm,* I felt good fortune
    as if I'd seen a unicorn. Nobody was around
      to laugh and say I'd not been briefly
    visited by a walking legend, a beast
  supremely itself, some dark and brilliant
king or queen of the underworld.

Near Pizza Plus he parked his body on cement steps.
In a drafty house, stories went, he drank lysol
like milk. Bony arms and caved-in shoulders hinted
how much he ate. A few times he snarled curses
as we walked by, but when our son was weeks old
Charlie bent over and touched his forehead
with a blackened, wrinkled finger, blessing him.

His one song was "How Great Thou Art."
Watering zucchini, picking up cigarette wrappers blown
in from the street, we figured singing at top volume
powerful and trembling and in-tune
might be his deepest pleasure (not that we knew
much about him or his pleasures). In the weeks
before the news noted his death, we heard him
so often his voice got entangled in the garden,
that hymn coming from afar
                    like a voice belonging to the wind.

Once I stood on a ladder sawing branches off
to keep our maple from the clothesline
and heard Charlie's voice grown louder, as if his words
rose higher than ever into the sky.
Back on earth, I wondered what his Great Thou
might be other than a lord and saviour:

his first breakfast in a week or two,

the sun's warmth on his long arms and long face
while he watched the spectacle of the street,

the strength he felt filling the neighbourhood
with his voice, the vibrato of his baritone
absorbed by everyone's flowers.

GRAVEYARD HAIKU

Walking, watch car lights
    sweep the night and pick out
this tombstone, then that

                    Black flecks crisscrossing
                        a pale headstone, ants
                    crawl in the cracks of a name

A prime minister's grave –
    century-old, pollen-dotted
target of wingseeds

                    A Celtic cross sports
                        a ski-hat. Was the joker from
                    this side of the grave, or that?

Far off, bagpipes – music
    these stones might make,
rolling out the exit

                    An obscure scurrying
                        rattles a branch – a red squirrel
                    on an angel's wing

I push the stroller over
    tombstone shadows. My son
wakes up and blinks

TREE TRILOGY

1

Twisted, cormorant-shaped, a spruce
has fastened itself to a thin ledge of cliff

high above waves that are calm
one day, furious and spattering the next.

One would think the basalt
as unwelcoming as a desert drowning

in sand, but the tree's needles
stay green, there where the salt wind

seasons it day after day;
and when the tide is highest

the waves – re-forming the rocks too slowly
for sight – climb to within inches of it,

then graze on the exposed, tentacle roots.
Ironrootus evergreen,

tenacitus cliffdweller. Slanted, half-way
to crawling juniper, it stretches outward

more than upward. A man lost there
would feel he was suspended

above some abyss, holding onto sanity
by his fingertips, soon to fall or die

of fright. The tree doesn't break its hold
and its seeds scatter

in the winds that keep it small and low.

2

Near midnight, wind-flung, a black branch
bends from its trunk to a street light
and hits. On a sidewalk by rain-sodden
Citadel Hill, where no windows shed
beams, a man under the skeletal elm
picks up his speed –
branch and light might break
aiming wood, bolts, and glass
at his streaming hair, his wet coat;

but he keeps casting a look behind
and up, where the flailing branch
batters the metal shield
until that light flutters and starts
to dim. Swaying harder and
harder, it knocks and knocks until
the light pales further and finally
(he glances over his shoulder)

goes out. To see the branch *do* that
gladdens him. The rain
keeps the stars at bay
and a minor stretch of the street
opens to a thicker darkness
unlit by electricity or artifice.

3

When the bookshelves are finally
in place, sparkling threads of sap
ooze from one of the boards.
Even the young carpenter is surprised

how the pine, kiln-dried at great heat,
still releases its vital flowing.
The sap isn't like sweat or blood
on a saintly stone forehead –

nobody has been thinking perfection
and lavish sacrifice.
I speak of my grandfather's mill,
the scrap boards he gave us to play with.

The smell of sawdust will always
mean him. As the young stranger packs up
his tools, he laughs, "Tap those shelves
next spring." The sap creeping over book covers

is like traces of a once relentless river,
a last wish before all wishes end,
my grandfather's breath rasping again
just when we were sure he was gone.

HAWTHORNDEN
IMPROVISATIONS

HAWTHORNDEN IMPROVISATIONS

Drafted during a month at Hawthornden Castle
International Retreat for Writers, Scotland, autumn 1996

Green surrounding the castle presses on every sense.
I came without much of a plan except to come without
much of a plan. In a month I'll be gone. September's
still young, not yet sloping toward October. Open eyes,
open ears. Through the window the days will slip

a few gifts, which I'll pick up thankfully, tinker with,
then hand on. I've sent no list of what I want,
the old image-bank is closed. "Improvisation
is the name of the game," I vowed to write
months ago, in winter, walking slippery streets of home

an ocean away. But the mole that burrows
surfaces, and I won't plug the hole if it crawls out.
The towns nearby want nothing from us.
"Have lived here me whole life," confessed a woman
selling me stamps, "and I've never heard of Haw –"

Layered leaves, distance, a dip downward
hide the castle from traffic, no sign but PRIVATE
hangs from the gates. Caves, cliffs, river, gorge,
footpath, fence, stile. Rosewell, Lasswade, Rosslyn,
Polton Bank, Bonnyrigg. Statue, plaque, turret, casement,

window, great door. Table, chair, bookcase, towels,
bed, mirror. Wren, rabbit, crow, dove, owl, badger,
Carlos, Gohar, Jim, Marina, Mary, Brian
(obscure as the bats in their caves),
sycamore, yew, beech, birch, oak, ash, holly.

*

There's the *dramatis personae*. Or a bit of it.
Invisible filaments from this small "I"
graze a cast of billions, by roads and ditches, in fields
and churchyards, under bridges and over hills and finally
wherever a thought can fly. What gets in is a smidgen,

a thumbnail playbill. By the footpath to Bonnyrigg,
past purple knapweed going to seed, howling
kennelled dogs added teeth to the afternoon peace.
One Easter, our housekeeper says over breakfast,
a priest handed out fluffy-feathered squirming chicks

to the children. Did he count how many peeped their last
in shoeboxes and baskets before the week was out?
He wasn't that different from most of us –
makers of symbols, our forgetful hands crushing
what they hold. With all that space, fields stretching away

to the Pentlands, litanies of ear-pleasing names –
Howgate, Leadburn, Peebles – why do I turn
to the boxed chick, the caged dog,
a hedgehog flattened like a spiny frisbee,
its guts gone? I'm handed all this freedom like a feast

but shove the platter aside to study bread and water.
Then what of the horses beyond the footpath
running, ripple-muscled, all strength and grace?
A mind needs freedom so much it turns a blind eye
to harnesses and stalls, and for one giddy moment

invents the last wild prehistoric horses of Scotland.
Lapwings shifted over bare soil, loosely flapping wide,
wide black-and-white wings in the wind
like structures almost coming unstrung but always keeping
together in the end, the whole creature excited and intact.

*

From the 1650's, Weenix's *Allegory of the Senses* has faced
a scattered fate. *Smell* I saw the other day in Edinburgh,
Hearing hangs in a gallery in Ohio, *Taste* and *Sight*
in the lobby of a New York hotel – and years ago *Touch*
vanished. Where can we hear tales of that family,

those quintuplets torn apart? How long have they languished
apart? Do they ever get back together? While we ate
crackers and biting-back cheddar, smelled and heard
logs burning nearby, I lifted an ancient lute from the wall
so Gohar, blind, could run her fingers over its slim neck,

half-pear body, worn pegs, and comically loose strings –
all its music translated into shape.
She traced the smoothnesses and the roughnesses,
histories of sounds and essences of light wood
drawn into her fingers. Reluctant to let it go,

forgetting her tea and cheese, she called the lute "beautiful."
In the candlelight, on the spot where the dusty instrument
had kept the wallpaper clean, *Touch*
seemed to float. So what, if *Sight* gets lost between trains
or stolen between planes, or turns out to be a forgery.

*

All the way to Dunbar a dog stank up the bus, its unmistakable
self spreading through the air like a furry signature.
The driver, harrumphing, stalked back to crank open
a roof vent. I gulped down fresh air, yet felt fond
of a country where the rankest mongrels ride buses.

In Dunbar, sea air blew the smell from my clothes.
Swooping martins cut instantly lost patterns through the air.
Wagtails lived up to their names, like marionettes
jerked by strings

              – marionettes? Leaping straight up
off the grass, they flicked their tails high, revelling

in what looked like play. No cloud-hidden Puppet Master
ruled over the North Sea, the upthrust outcroppings
of rock. No Lord or Lady with strings pulled the waves
back and forth, made the redshank peck wet sand.
However small, each thing fed from its own nature,

inflamed with energies like the logs now burning
in the fireplace at my back. *Crack!* one goes, shooting a cinder
against the grate. When I curved down the sloping road
inside the gates, dusk smudged everything into half-light,
thick limbo. Dozens of rabbits bolted and scattered,

an owl called its three-part question three times
in three minutes. No puppeteer switched on the lights
in the castle windows, no strings lifted my feet.
The rabbits and the owl drank from the pools
called *rabbit* and *owl*. *Crack!* goes another log at my back.

                          *

I thought the Old World knew nothing of "wilderness"
but all day I find woods and glens where shade
only lets in slivers of light, tree trunks stretch wider
than Little John's arms, ivy thrives everywhere, and
the vegetation even bites. What kind of nettle or thorn

stabs bare legs, but only leaves invisible stings?
I'd rather see welts or blood, know an honest plant
when I bump into one. Itching, thirsty, I reached a chapel
where masons' labours have long been silent
but ageless sprouting and blooming are fixed in over-

flowing Gothic stonework. Carved lilies, daisies, roses
crowd the ceiling, and hart's tongue fern, cactus, sweetcorn
climb the walls and pillars, while green men blend in, vines
and leaves jutting from their mouths, crossing
their cheeks and ears. Motionless, camouflaged,

many of those pagan faces are tricky to pick out.
Like owls hidden in the day, they watched us
while we walked past, blind. Some stranger guessed,
"A maniac with a chisel just kept going, and couldn't stop."
If so, give me such mania, to chisel words like roots and petals,

hoping our homes won't be blighted and abstract,
the walls blank but for our own concoctions
ignorant of pistils and anthers. Rosslyn Chapel even
made me grateful for the stings I kept rubbing,
those fiery needle-pierces.

A rusty ladder leads down
into Hawthornden's dungeon,
down into stale, still air.
Our narrow-beamed flashlight
strikes no moss, no water,

no bones. Nothing tells
of whoever groaned and bled
here. Nothing moves
but one spider, butternut-coloured, fleeing
the lightbeam. Fast as a swallow

to a fly, my eyes go to a tunnel
cut through walls eight-feet thick –
a barred opening
onto light-soaked leaves and trees.
From this bland dankness

that bright green is
incomparable –
like a patch of rare abundance
if the earth dwindled some day
to a half-baked disaster,

a range of few species.
What does the rain-fed
crammed-with-trees glen hint
of razed hedgerows, birdless fields,
seeds withering on metal?

In the dungeon's dank
the tunnel's opening hangs
suspended, iron bars across leaves.
My hands itch to thrust out
reaching and twisting for a touch.

*

Hence it was that although he could not read, he would turn
over and examine books which she used either for her devo-
tions or her study, and whenever he heard her express liking
for a particular book, he would also look at it with special in-
terest, kissing it and often taking it into his hands.

– Turgot, confessor of Margaret,
wife of Malcolm III of Scotland (1057–93)

Tell me no more about the king, for just that image
is enough: Ceann-Mor, "Great Chief," willing to play the clown
for love, a man touching a book with his lips
as if it were Margaret's child born before they met –
and the child chatters to her but always stays mute

around Stepfather. Paint me that. Push aside sword fights,
beheadings and flag-raisings, rush through the public square
and go find the man alone inspecting a book loved
by his beloved. How many of us have done much the same,
staring at strangenesses fathomed by the one we adore?

Forget it was a castle, forget he was a king.
Be careful not to startle him by touching his shoulder
or clearing your throat. *Don't* paint that moment,
its privacy is so great. Knowing he asked artisans
to adorn her favourite books with gold and gems

adds nothing. Once again, merely picture him kissing
a cover – as I today kissed a letter from home,
though I'm luckier than the Ceann-Mor
because I can read the words and they
(never-ending astonishment) were written to me, for me.

*

At the roadside on the edge of Rosewell, a startling heap
blocked a walker's way. Striped shirts, lipstick tubes,
a blue dress, a yardstick, a stuffed bear, light bulbs
in their boxes, letters in their envelopes, family photos
stranded among the rocks and dirt. No garbage,

this heap had a look of having belonged to a home
just hours earlier, affections still clinging to it
like perfume to a misplaced coat. Wrapped candies spilling
from a bowl, onto a cat calendar. Who had flung it all
down, pouring curses on top? Who had given up on talk,

grabbed whatever was near and carried it in a car trunk
to that lonely spot? When I returned in the evening
the jumble was gone, like blood stains washed away.
Maybe a statement had been made, the scene wound down
with tears and kisses. Maybe the blue dress

was back on its hanger, the letters in their drawer.
Maybe. Caught in overhanging brambles, a missed photo:
a couple smiling like a million others. I heard
silence holding a house in its grip and, ticking,
skipping beats, another event waiting to happen.

*

Dearest K. – Everywhere today lacked you. The leafiness
would've been leafier, the glen's deep wetness
wetter, if you'd been there. In no time you'd warm up
this chilled room, putting my poem out in the hall
like the laundry bag or the lunch basket

and guiding me from the desk, across the room.
In caves under the castle, families in animal skins
set up house back in the Bronze Age. Imagine us
then and there – berry-eating, bad-toothed troglodytes.
Once I've laughed such fantasies away,

sometimes it *does* seem we knew each other
in another life and felt, then too, as much happiness
as anyone has reason to hope for.
To lessen separation by an ocean, I try
to think only of your eyes. In museums, alone,

I've wanted you to see the elephant's-ear sponge,
the pelican's-foot shell, the staircase abalone –
once at home and lapped in their elements, now
even their sad labelled selves worth witnessing
for you! This far away, I can hardly bear to remember

your body, your fingers unlocking
door after door after door. Should I scribble
"Variations on 'jumping your bones' "?
But when your breasts are in my hands
it's not bones I'm thinking of, if I'm thinking at all.

*

Another quiet day. Frustrated pockets of air barked and
    pounded
in the pipes. At breakfast Jim talked about his hip giving out
and anti-inflammatory pills with the strength of 18 aspirins.
Carlos's characters begged to be heard. Rooks gathered
and rasped, tempting groundskeepers to reach for their guns.

A dead branch fell into the river, scattering the trout.
Another quiet day. Marina scrutinizes cults obsessed
with the end of the world, so Doom's Day flickered
around our dinner talk. Pens and keyboards scratched and clicked
like spirits under the floorboards, fighting

to escape. Past midnight, in my room's pitch black,
Duke's orchestra filled the walkman with more pitches
than I could count: "Way Early Subtone," "Hero to Zero,"
"Low Key Lightly," "Upper and Outest." Another
quiet day.

                              *

Woke up and for a few moments this was no castle
but an overheated rink full of folding chairs
and faceless strangers whispering like the ocean,
waiting for me to tear myself from sleep. A thin girl leaned
closer, telling me it was time to deliver the sermon,

but I'd forgotten, I had no notes, and stage fright
shook me from head to foot … For a week
when ten, I wanted to be an evangelist,
not an astronaut or hockey star. Decades later
that always gets a good laugh around the table.

What won me over the night I watched the famous preacher
in the rink? The power to pick up a heart and stroke it?
His gestures rising and falling? His tale-telling?
His voice moulding language like clay?
Soon enough the pulpit shrank

to a stick of firewood, but I never stopped hearing
words thaw, slide, cascade. Even in that echoing rink
what I wanted wasn't hammered into stone
but flowing like water through a gorge
down embankments and over rocks and around bends.

*

Sources of the trite – the rose, the rainbow – won't go away.
They stay stubbornly themselves, not bothering to glance
at the medallions we stamp them on, the songs we slip them in.
From Edinburgh Castle's extinct volcanic mound, high over the city
and the Firth of Forth, today's arc stretched, deepest-coloured,

miles wide, like the original rainbow – the impossible-to-achieve
form for all others. Inside, stained glass was merely exquisite,
even the day's other surprise: a Navy Memorial window
with its swarming marginalia of octopi and squid,
bits of the spectrum scattered through treacherous waters.

*

The Keep Library stands above the dungeon,
a head above a withered, paralyzed body.
From a high shelf, Shelley's "The Defence of Poetry"
reads: "When composition begins, inspiration is already
on the decline." But from this desk, the ideal poem

drifting somewhere out there before the words arrive
is pie-or-poppycock-in-the-sky, a featureless face
or less, a blankness where a face might form.
Sometimes the real thing starts breathing only minutes
or hours after the first hesitant line,

when the horse's blood has warmed up
after days in the stable, sullenly munching the hay.
Then you're in the fields or on the hills, gulping
the blood-nourishing air, and anything can happen.
There's not much I'm rock-solid sure of, but I'd swear

the river in the glen isn't mimicking a crystal river
smoothly rushing in a perfect place; the ivy isn't
secondhand ivy, climbing a secondhand tree;
and the rabbits aren't overshadowed by rabbits
whose digestion is instant, who drop no shit pellets

onto impossibly green grass. From the lunch basket,
the sandwich bread is a bit stale, the peach crushed
in one spot – but it's a peach, lush in my mouth.
In the library, the butterfly that landed on book spines
had tattered wings, holes in its gold and black.

*

If you play that fiddle, really play it. Dance your fingers
and the bow over the strings as if it's your last chance.
No tame, proper toeing of the melodic line, please.
Fracture the scales, spin the sharps and flats,
bring them back to rest. If you don't dig in

like the skilled ones branded the devil's fiddlers,
why play at all? Or so I told myself coming back on a bus,
ringing from a ceilidh in the city. But beside me
a drunk stranger with a bald, pink head nodded off
and missed his stop. This can happen:

the rivers all become sluggish, the horses all lame,
and exhaustion with everything muffles all music
into one temptation: *Stop your heartbeat. End it all.*
I'm very far from the first girl I told "I love you,"
awkwardly, looking past her, on a bridge long since

torn down. Over two years we talked hundreds of hours
but hardly touched, though I dreamed of it daily
and wrote her labyrinthine letters and worshipful poems
comparing her words to wingseeds, punning on her name,
until all that teenage yearning ended

around the time I saw with distaste that she, a shy girl,
was wearing blue nail-polish. Later such pettiness
shamed me: to feel blue nail-polish meant that much!
When I opened a *Gleaner* to her cryptic obituary,
for twenty years we'd not shared a moment,

a word. Why did I instantly guess right? I'll never know
why she found her last act irresistible …
what she filled her second twenty years with …
who found her first – sprawled, or bent in her final slump …
whether I'm a ghoul to wonder.

*

These mornings over breakfast and newspapers
are we pampered dogs on the hearth hung with black pots,
drooling over scraps? When castles were young
they shut out hungry, scar-faced strangers dressed in rags.
Some days this seems a stone-hearted shelter.

The girl with "a voice of handbells" became a woman
and I heard no more of her until she cut her ties
to the earth. Long ago those tempting, taunting scissors
appeared to me, in a cloud but clear;
then I'd wake up one morning sooner or later

to the odd, unexpected comfort of some small thing –
a many-veined leaf sealed in amber-like ice,
a few syllables by Issa about an insect –
and wonder if I were sick not to feel sicker.
Maybe it's a lucky gene that makes some of us

clutch any small mercy tightly, lifted away
from ourselves toward a stray bar of music
in the wind, or a view of the North Sea from a train
like a vista of promised water and sky
that gives despair, like the oak and the plum tree, a place.

*

For the luckiest, Nothingness never points the way,
a bottomless pond never pulls at their feet.
For the unluckiest, Nothingness gives off tempting scents
and if they choose it, maybe *that* is something,
all they have. But who can celebrate the end of all change

for them? Don't ask the bus driver helping a one-legged woman
aboard, the hornet circling blackberry jam, the grocer unlocking
his shop, sniffing new weather, a degree cooler or warmer,
a notch dryer or wetter. They're not yet ready
for the whiteness at the core of whiteness.

When I recall those whose landscapes are slashed,
face down on the floor, the vista that reached out to me
becomes little more than quaint needlework.
When I vowed to improvise, I predicted fiddling
different tunes on different days, but now the bow keeps

going to the same spot. Imagine tapping human will
into the energy of a bird the weight of two quarters
that flies all the way from Glasgow to Cape Town –
what would that mean to someone with no will
left? Talk like that could wound the wounded.

Should I put a blank page here,

                                   an hour of silence?

I'm afraid
there's little to say ...
All the way to Bonnyrigg and back, this afternoon

I fought windy buffets, strained knees, a wobbly-
wheeled bicycle. Though not much happened
stories started to seem timelier than arguments:
Once there was a cyclist whose feet could hardly
reach the pedals, who knew he would disappear

if he climbed off ... Once there was a knight alive
at the wrong time, and his horse led him to a cliff ...
Once there was walker who fell into brambles,
their berries blackening his shirt like bloodstains.
Though no cuts showed, he burned at countless points ...

*

Too many recent days, I've treated what's out there
like dessert – any walk on the Castle Path
can tell me that, deep-streaked cliffs rearing overhead,
unidentified calls all around – but you can't expect
endless revelations, some days you need to stand back

and let everything go on its way, unpilfered,
unexamined, caught up in its own weavings and dodgings.
If the day seems a void, an empty sky, the past can fill it
with clouds splitting apart or pulling together. Hidden,
camouflaged, packed in by the dozen, rooks erupted

from the tree tops. Their response to my footsteps
stopped me, as if a hundred voices inside me answered
like wings lifting. No curtains close as I keep building
a record of minor moments, accidents and hopes.
The cook is in the garden, pulling up roots

for supper. I'm still figuring out where waking reaches
its peak, and tuning my nerves to others,
a swarming behind the leaves. At the desk I look up
and hear something – a cry bending into a squawk,
just that, once – and I answer it without speaking.

A WORLD OF COUNTING

WORK AT TWENTY-ONE

1

That spring, nothing pleased him more than reaching
the riverside gallery hours before it opened,
the statues on the green returning to daylong sleep,
morning like a lavish breakfast prepared for him alone.

Alone as a ship's dawn watch, he erased traces
of the previous day, rubbing windowcleaner over prints
pressed onto the front doors. Guiding a mop across
sunlit floors, he wordlessly greeted familiar scenes –
a stone bridge arching like a pebbled mouth,
an actress flattered as angel-flanked St.Cecilia,
a feast with grapes, goblets, apple-cheeked revellers
and glazed pig. Some mornings he ran fast and
slid, the mop a dishevelled hockey-stick.
Once when a lord and lady surveying their estate grew
more masterful before his eyes, he stuck out his tongue,
then waited for their hound to leap from the canvas.

He poured hissing disinfectant into toilets, stirred
with a brush, but only years later thought,
"I turned the water a Gainsborough blue."

It was still an age of typewriters and cigarettes.
Half the writers in the tabloid office smoked,
ash trays filled with butts by mid-day. Coughing,
he proofread in a room of small smoulderings.

Having stripped tape from crates of art, he now
opened giant envelopes. His ballpoint hovered
above the short paragraphs, out for blood
– transposed letters, wrong date, missing phrase.
Experts announced foolproof preventions for cancer

and the common cold, a woman who'd slept twenty years
woke up and thought it was still her wedding day,
a human-dog language was invented, aliens
burned the shape of a cross into a cornfield.

If he made too many mistakes *not* finding mistakes,
the axe would fall. Every few hours the scowling editor
emerged and circulated, his face greasy
like the unlucky pig's, his reputation for ruthlessness
hanging like other smoke from the floresence.

From 9 to 5, the proofreader hunted all-too-human
lapses – a beach cleaner relieved to spear
scraps of garbage amidst tedious expanses of sand.
Each evening he threw a smoky shirt in the laundry
like cotton tainted by the smell of error.

3

On an X-ray department's night shift, he ended work
around the hour he'd cleaned the gallery doors.
In the green smock of an "untrained attendant" he
    wheeled
patients from floor to floor; slipped heavy cassettes
into pillowcases, lifted the strangers high enough
to slide the cushioned metal under their backs;
dropped rolled film down old pneumatic tubes
to the processing room – a hissing, a rumbling,
sounds of hope and misery falling through
the guts of a building like an ailing body.

Straining after words muffled by a plastic mask,
he managed small talk about a recent blizzard,
a hockey fight. X-rays complete, Mr. Finestone's smile
nudged beyond the corners of his mask, then he raised
one hand in a V-for-Victory as if to say,
"Don't panic, son – we do what work
we can, and small wins are better than none."

The next night Mr. Finestone's face went blue, then grey.
The young man in the thready smock retreated
to the windows, useless, his hands pocketed to keep
from shaking, the view blocked by nurses and doctors
and machines, sudden thirst drying out his throat.
He'd never before stood in a room where death
climbed triumphantly atop another and crowed.

On the way home, he saw dirty snowbanks turning
into pale corpses in the gaps between street lights.
Sleepless in bed, he searched the want ads and noted
a printer's mistake and feared work would never again
offer the unbroken egg of a perfect morning.

THREE WINDOWS

In a blue-shuttered house high on a hill
his first window faced a band of blue water
a mile away. From the eyrie of the top bunk
he watched the city and the river while he rested
on his side like a river, turning buildings sideways.

His desk, defined by a pencil line dividing his half
from his brother's, stretched under the window.
Upriver was his brother's half; downriver,
his. Some days, edging toward dream, his elbows
stationed on a worn blotter, he lifted his chin to gaze
down over tree-hidden streets, train tracks, steeples,
bridges; he never imagined sitting at another desk
and scanning vistas from under a rooftop
in that valley, in another life. One sudden spring
ice thawed and flooded the windowsill, dripping
down onto books lining the back of his desk.

*

In a city big enough to enfold his native place
fifty times, his second bedroom was his one room,
a basement cave, grasses speared against a window
leading to an alleyway – faceless brick, winding
wrought-iron fire-escapes, sparrows flicking
old toast around garbage cans. For years he lived
alone, sometimes eating a plate of macaroni
or a bowl of stew at his table facing the window.

Swaddled in sweaters in the chill, he recalled
obeying family calls to supper and needing
headphones to hear his music. Fewer rules
tied him down now, but when he travelled by train
along dull sluggish waterways, memory made
that first river wider and more gracefully curved:
once taken in stride, like parents' love, it took on
a new blueness, and its banks grew greener than before.

*

Another decade, another city, he wakes
to colliding sounds – foghorn, gull. If he'd heard them
from the bedroom on the hill, he would've known
he was adrift, a boy on a continent breaking its contours.
Through the blinds he sees a garden and, behind that,
a graveyard. Lilac blossoms have scattered over
his childrens' plastic wagons, but summer's not half gone.
Tombstone names mumbled on his walks home
– ALLSOP, WAMBOLT, CROOK, BARNSTEAD –
surface from his sleep to be mouthed.

Comparing three bedrooms from his life, he ignores
a dozen others. Three is a handy number
and all stories use scissors. Once he didn't dream
of walking around in another body, yet now he gropes
for bits of days when he never paid a penny
for shelter and food, and his name never sounded
alien. He sees the years as a blend of chance
and mischance, scribblings by wild fateful hands.

On his most recent visit to his first house, he forgot
to walk upstairs and gaze out the window he once knew
so well. But last week he read a book he'd postponed
knowing for thirty years. Its rough pages were rippled
as if once dipped in the waters of a river.

AFTER THE AGE OF PARTIES

So slowly has he crept into middle age
he can't pinpoint when the parties of his youth
became distant and dream-like, reflections
on rain-smeared windows. It was in another city
he lived alone through his twenties, gathering
odd jobs like a collector of postponed futures,
cycling through dangerous streets with few thoughts
of danger, tending nothing but cacti in small apartments.

When the smell of spring mud rose from alleyways
and invaded balconies, or when snow puddled
by boots at the door, he improvised zigzag courses
among friends and strangers, eyeing happiness
as explorers eye mountaintops from level land.
In a fiddler's kitchen, he played the spoons until two Irishmen
mocked his rhythms. Later at a Greek bodega, backed
into a corner with no easy exit, he walked across the table
past candles and jugs of sangria, and a waiter threatened
to throw him out. Some nights in murky diningrooms
near furniture hulked like shapes in catacombs
he danced until his glasses slipped down his nose,
hair sweat-jagged. One such night he laughed
at a rich girl gathering her empties to take home
so her dad could cash them in, and she lashed out,
"Nosey bastard!" Stung, he retreated to the balcony;
a voice from a car jeered, "*Sautez, mon ami!*"

He saw himself as a Beast with no Beauty;
a skulking, timid tom in a pack of cats.
Some nights when he walked home, sirens shrieked
their melodrama over rats' tails of drenched grass.
Uniformed door-men he glimpsed through glass
were statues he wanted to smash. Women's faces
were already filling up his memory,
the forests of their hair waving.

In a smaller city, as he drops another log
into his wood stove and reads a book about dragons
to his daughters,
                    laughter out on the street
hints at those nights when the great city
spiralled into his eyes, and he tried a drink called
Moscow Mule, and he felt a ridiculous triumph
on his doorstep, dazed and lonely, finding the right key.

Parties that flickered with hope often ended
with wishes for healing oblivion. Yet he catches
a bit, a spark – faded but glowing – of nights
whirlwinds scattered promises around his feet
while taxis nosed their way through labyrinths
and headlights shone on the mountain like comets.

Every lion until now was sun-faced, lacy-maned,
a Leo with beaming eyes and no hint of claws.
A child who first walked ten months ago
learns the word "dark," giving the "d" and the "k"
their full force. Now he says "lion"
with his voice shaking, his lip lowered
in fear, and the lion and the dark go together.

He sees a beast in the unlit confusion below
the basement stairs, under the rocking chair
by his costume box, in the shadowed
distances of the study. His parents can't say
how the soft-pawed creature changed overnight
any more than how the first manticore
stalked into some mind aeons ago.
Maybe one day the child looked into a mirror
and saw the darkness behind his own teeth;
maybe all of a sudden he heard
the danger in his own comical roar. Fear
is more than a taste he doesn't like,
more than a strategy to get his way. Weeks ago
the first slap of ocean waves against his legs
made him whimper and ask to be held.

The father thinks: *The dark needs a body,*
the lion serves the purpose. It seems some maw
opens and opens and would swallow
all – boy, room, house. When their son runs
to their legs, the parents look into the obscurity
he shows them, and they glimpse again
the breeding cave of their own dread,
a source nothing on earth lights up.

A GLOSA FOR JOSHUA

You will come to a place where the streets are not marked.
Some windows are lighted. But mostly they're darked.
A place you could sprain both your elbow and chin!
Do you dare to stay out? Do you dare to go in?
> Dr. Seuss, *Oh, The Places You'll Go!*

I've waited two years to write you some lines
– nothing you'll read for a very long time.
Past midnight I picture you wrestling these words
at twelve or twenty, when you might ask the page,
"Who were you talking to when I was just two?"
One day when you ask what it would've been like
if the land were the ocean and the ocean the land,
if your mother and I never boarded one boat,
if the dogfish all meowed and the catfish all barked,
you will come to a place where the streets are not marked.

Riddles of the what-if and the never-was
crawl in from the sea like Edinburgh mist,
mist of the castled city where we first gave you
a chance to be. To imagine you now as not
is to face a blank like no other blank,
to pause and stumble, bereft and shocked.
When we lead ourselves by the nose into dreams
that this or that never was – candles, mirrors,
hopes, regrets, the red-throated loon, the great auk –
some windows are lighted. But mostly they're darked,

and if we stand there too long we grow cold.
When you're forty-something, my age tonight,
will I be a scattering of ashes? – (taboo:
father hints of his own x). Near the harbour shops,
where you call a lobster trap and a dreamcatcher
basketball nets, we see one boat named VIM
and one named VIGOUR. Some day we'll learn
to laugh at the grave and trip up ogres
by making bad jokes, like calling a coffin
a place you could sprain both your elbow and chin.

The child you are and the man you will be
blend into each other, back and forth
– back and forth, the child you are and the infant
you were. The first morning that rises without me
will be bright compared to your never having been.
In Scotland there was a b & b, and in the b & b
your mother and I imagined a door, and on the door
your face was sketched in invisible ink. That night
we entered and left in the dust the questions
"Do you dare to stay out? Do you dare to go in?"

SICK FOR THE NEW MILLENNIUM

December 31, 1999-
January 1, 2000

A man overcome with raw throat, backache,
feverish cheeks and forehead
clung to home and felt like doing nothing.
Each trip down to the kitchen
like a child learning stairs
he gripped the bannister with one hand.

As year folded into year, with blankets to his chin
he watched torches tossed high in New Zealand,
waltzes spun in the streets of Vienna, mallet music
hammered between ice walls above the Arctic Circle.
Fireworks chainlinked China – Paris –
London – the Grand Parade a mile from his couch.
Did he want to be out there? He couldn't say
for sure – but when strangers in far-flung cities pointed
microphones at shrieking crowds and asked,
"Having *funnnn?*" he almost bit his blankets.

Red-nosed, he pressed his face to a window
above the back yard: no celebrating flowers sprung up
out of season, no beasts strayed from the woods
to watch explosions and sniff the sizzled air.
The trees stood there as usual, changing
imperceptibly, no calendars in their branches.

74

In bed he thought of his son, new to speech,
chanting excitedly, "One two eight six!"
Once numbers had charmed him too
with their novelty, useful for pigs, balloons, and blocks
but not yet for years, whatever years were
(the days more than enough).

Reaching through the dark for his glass of water,
he wished this night were to him as it was
to the mice in the walls, the whales off the coast –
a time unique as any; yet he was trapped
in a world of counting, where years are added up
like spoons and fingers and pages. Until he slept
he felt numbers falling upon him,
falling upon him
like a whisper of data, a dark blizzard of ashes.

DINER IN A STORM

Far across town from the take-outs and food courts
snow against the windows of a small diner
snaps, ticks. One grey-haired waitress serves all.
Around the U-shaped counter, twenty swivel
stools are filled. High on the walls,
rows of decorated plates – a turkey gobbler,
the hills of Cape Breton edging the sea,
Shakespeare's weary-eyed face crowning a map
of Stratford-upon-Avon. The fries are as pale
as the waitress's face; lakes of butter float
atop the chowder. Three green-smocked cleaning ladies
tip their chins high, savour their smoke rings.
Another regular, coat collar up, gives himself
over to a triangle of lemon pie, meringue
grizzling his moustache. Lady Di in pink looks down
upon them all – she was up there even before
the fatal crash. Here you find men from the docks
resting their heavy arms, a Taj Mahal no bigger
than a coffee pot, and two stuffed bull-dogs –
parent and pup – on the arborite counter by the cash.

THREE TALES OF HALIFAX

1

To the nerve-banging music of ailing radiators,
a family of five struggled from their beds.
Tired of *things,* they slept restlessly
all night, as if vans of *things* were unloaded into
their heads, leaving no room for peace and dreams.
Spring seemed frozen forever in memory,

so after breakfast they set up shelves and cardtables
on the snowy sidewalk. Chipped dishes,
T-shirts from concerts by forgotten bands,
a board-hockey game with earthquake splits
down its ice, a stuffed bear named "Jasper"
from Jasper, a seashell necklace, a whale's tooth …

Nobody came. Up and down the street,
behind curtained and frosted windows, neighbours
fondled or questioned last week's presents. White
started to fall, burying the metal hockey-players
and rising like sea foam over the seashell necklace.
The youngest child looked up and told the snow,
"You can have everything. Take it."

Hours later when they stepped back outside
the tables were bare but for the snow,
which had grown plumper, tumbling onto the cars.

2

At midnight, over puddle-streaked floors
by bank machines, white slips – boot-marked,
helter-skelter. To a shivering woman unzipping
her purse, all that abandoned data stirred up longings
for exchanges of beads or shells. Strewn
like wingseeds, the slips deepened her loneliness
a few degrees. She punched buttons, the beeping
like mockery. When she shouldered the door open
against a snowdrift, wind picked up the slips
and carried them spinning down the street.

Later she floundered through a dream's blizzard
to a circle of new trees, the night's crop,
a celebration of ice hanging from branches.

3

Walking home from shopping on the coldest,
windiest day of winter, a man and a woman said
nothing about sales. The man told the woman,
"This morning I learned the word 'inglenook.'"

The Public Gardens were a private haven for snow and ice.
In the whirl, parking meters were alien statues
near obliteration; hotels, simplified by white,
looked like penitentiaries; neon smudged.

"… a corner by a fireplace," said the man,
ice in his beard, "a shelter for rest and warmth."
She wondered aloud if only the rich were so lucky,
if even lowly kitchens housed such comforts –
rug, simmering stew, sparks cracking. "Inglenook,"
she said, a white scarf up to her eyes, "inglenook …

inglenook … ," until her chant became a niche –
bare but radiant – and the way her mouth
made the word warmed him
on their slow return through the wind and snow.

Atlas, we laughed, swallowed a pill
big as an Olympic discus. A basement coffee shop
hosted our first reunion in years – three friends
together for a few breaths, swapping stories
of medications, counsellors, side-effects (the price
of keeping chest pains and shortness of breath
at bay). We joked about Atlas shouldering
house sales, family visits, kids' trips to Emergency,
work politics, family dispersions. Oh the thunder
the great pill made plummeting down his throat!
The waiter caught the phrase "zilch libido"
and asked, "That the name of a new band, or what?"

"Under the weather"? – as if it were possible *not*
to be under weather, without warmth or cold,
dryness or wet. Neither sunlight nor rain would ever
fall from the sky. There would be no sky.
        No sky!

Comparing bad days and nights, we closed down
the coffee shop. Out on the sidewalk, we glanced
through the windows at our feet: three waiters
lifting chairs onto tables. What was it, subtle

as a drifting spot of pollen,
                              that calmed me
for the time it took to reach the parking lot?
Those strangers arranged the room with such speed,
such grace. They might've been raising my panic
above their shoulders, then setting it down
to balance in the dark for the rest of that night.

Day after day, I see more toe nails than eyes.
I'd push the truth if I said my office
is smaller than my patients' cardboard shelters,
but it's more cramped than most. The floor tiles curl
at the edges, the light bulbs are bare, and Hank
might hear Horace's cracking joints behind the screen.
Only a few old men call me "Ma'am," like I was
a teacher from their childhoods more distant
than death.
                Years ago when the devils of arthritis started
needling my feet, I withdrew from General Practice,
learned everything I could about ankles, heels, shins,
the metatarsal and the phalanges, the way a rabbi
dissects Deuteronomy. I've unknotted laces
that fell apart like spaghetti, peeled off
running shoes that erupted like abscesses.

More than shirts or hats, shoes tells stories –
of chafings and stumbles, a thousand weathers,
a schizophrenic's circular miles trod,
trod, trod. Famous footwear – Cinderella's,
Chaplin's – are odourless in the face of the real.
I've seen no feet I would dry with my hair.
They're the colour of mushrooms, wilted roses,
eggplant skin. Hands rubber-gloved, I swear
feet have voices, words arising from blisters

and broken flesh, not from mouths and beards.
Those voices tell me, mumbling or unexpectedly
clear, raspy or childlike, of frostbitten nights in parks,
skinhead stormtrooper boots, a door forced shut
where the clean and moneyed are wanted.

When the feet twitch with monologues, I can't get a word
in edgewise against the jagged curses and
laughter, all entangled with enemies and wraiths.
Then I feel like some doctor in hell, a fire
burning at my door. The poor and the miserable
were cast there not for punishment, but merely
by the whims of whatever does the casting.

Some nights at home, I stare at my feet
projecting beyond the tub's foam: afflicted
but lucky. Back on the street, the homeless might hobble
less, but trailing my fingers in lavender oil I ask
who will bandage their minds, who will pour ointment
onto their nerves? When I write out slips
for the pharmacy or the hospital, I'm never sure if
they'll reach other hands, or flutter down the sidewalk
in a wet wind. As I pull the plug of my bath,
I've pictured my prescriptions and referrals,
like prayers ending mid-sentence, sluiced away
                                        in the street's rain.

THE SONOGRAPHER

for Al Moritz

Call me Broadcaster of the Early Heartbeat,
First Examiner of the Head's Circumference,
He Who Sees Your Child First. Call me
young Mr. Faith, Mr. Hope. I could say:
"high-frequency sound waves going at
five-to-seven-million cycles per second."
A fine science, this. Most days it's business
as usual; but when the commonness of it all
subsides, for a few seconds it seems – dare I say –
sacramental, and I recall holding my wife's hand,
watching our son turn like a shadowy fish
on the screen (not "ghostly form,"
ghostliness being on the other side of life).

I'm the coroner's sunny double, his lucky brother.
Just once, I'd have us switch places
to spare him dark questions and bloody probings
for a night. I wonder if he'd bow
to the consummate promise of a fetus forming –
if he'd weep to be in my shoes.

Far from home, bubbled in vacation, I crave the time
when a shoulder or foot comes into view,
the opposite of dissolving. It gets addictive, this gentle
saying to strangers, "There it is – see?"
Once I sat all week on a Cuban beach with the sky
like an empty screen, and I would've been glad
to see a cloud as small as a kneecap.

The news, of course, isn't always cheering. Then
what I see straightens my mouth, tightens a knot
in my throat. I've jotted symbols you don't want
to grasp, but Drs. MacKeigan or Varma or Finch
deliver the news. I see, and say nothing, guilty
I'm spared the job. I've seen celebration drain
from eyes in an instant, then a week later
struggle back, stubborn, giving a welcome at last.
"Sweet one," they whisper, "… angel."

Who can *see* hope more clearly than I, day
after day? – a shadowy head turning this way,
a thumb going to a mouth, like a joke
at our gazing, our impatience. I'm one of fate's
surveyors. Maybe it's a right no one
should have – to be an eavesdropper on the future,
always the first on board to spot
a thin beautiful line of land barely lifting
                        above the horizon and the sea.

TALKING TO THE BIRDS

TALKING TO THE BIRDS

> ... one's cry of O Jerusalem becomes little by little
> a cry to something a little nearer and nearer until
> at last one cries out to a living name, a living
> place, a living thing.
>
> – Wallace Stevens, *Opus Posthumous*

1   to a red-eyed vireo

Minimalist of the tree tops,
more than a scrap of the dawn chorus, all day
you ask and answer one question
in two-to-four-note phrases, your drawl's inflections
reversing, a rise giving way to a fall, a fall
to a rise,

   ask, answer,

      ask, answer ...
Is it fair to say you sound like a lecturer who won't
move on to the next point,

       or some weary barker
slowly going mad with the monotony of selling?

"*Vireo* is Latin for *I am green*," I can say,
"your back is olive, your cap grey, you raise cowbirds
who squirmed and pushed your nestlings
to their deaths" –

     but how can I pretend to know

what you ask and answer? Or even
that you ask and answer anything?

From the highest leaf-hidden branches
your voice wriggles into my ear, turns more nerve-
rattling than any scream or shriek. If I blocked out
all the other notes in the woods and listened
only to yours, all day, every day, I might be the one
who slipped into the shadows forever

repeating the one thought I can't give up.

Fog like cold sweat coated every inch of the ferry,
swathed and hid the ocean ten feet out. Downstairs
indoors, passengers snacked, napped,
fought the warriors and demons of video games.

For those of us circling the deck
the first hour of the crossing didn't yield
one bird, one mewl or wayward cry. Grand Manan
could've been a mile off, or a thousand.
If allowed extravagance, I'd say
the waves peaked and toppled like the waves
                    in the story of the seven days
when "everything according to its kind"
was born. Then, you:
                    flying, unmistakable, goose-sized,
your butter-yellow head the one contrast
to all that pallor. Where everything else was wispy
and smudged, you were suddenness, otherness,
completeness,
eyes and beak and wingbeat.

Just as quickly, you slipped back behind
the gathering of spectres. When I pushed closer
against the cold iron railing
                    you were back with me,
then vanished again, like a feeling that keeps coming
and going on the verge of sleep.
For a minute you were the first bird, or the last.

At a field's far end where you roost in that bare tree,
your paleness fits into the level land –
ice spanning ditches, frost crystalling stubble,
snow heaped and spread over most memories of green.

No other hawk locks its talons to the branch you grasp
X number of miles and inches north of Wolfville,
south of Blomidon. Nothing else feathered or beaked
grabs the mouse and the mole you grab
at 10: 31 a.m., 2: 13 p.m.; no other's wheezy cry
whistles into the ears of a girl named Mary-Lou
and a skittish dog named Sebastian
in the split between the same two seconds.

But couldn't we say the same even if your back
were brown, your tail red? For praise,
wouldn't any other redtail do as well? –
your paleness just a sure way of saying
you are you, born at one moment and
dying at another, that pairing of moments

yours alone, singular
as the dance of a girl and a dog.

4   to a great blue heron

The comedy stops me: while two terns swoop at you
again and again, you don't gaze up at them once
yet with each obnoxious dive nearly grazing
your fine-feathered crest,
                              you duck,
keeping your wings still, drawing in your epic neck.
Warned by the whisper of each harassing rush,
you're the straight bird to their fooling around.

At the end of a trail smothered with goldenrod
and wild roses, once I suddenly broke through brush
and found a river with one of your kind
there, so close I watched its eye peeled for a flick
in the shallows. Wind stirred its slate-blue feathers,
then the great wings lifted like a recovered heartbeat
or the word *ahhhh.*
                         If gangly grace has always
been your middle name, this peskiness is a test.
I have to laugh, though no louder than a dragonfly,

as you dodge
another dive, refusing to move down the pond.

That is not you. It's a stuffed effigy. The deep
undulations of your flight were finished
decades ago. In the old glass cabinet, the silence
never ends. Wild canary, you no longer shake
thistledown to the earth, no longer sing
your descending notes as you follow your rolling
route through the air. That's not you, but a body
drained of blood – paralyzed force, gesture
without motion – the colour of withered dandelions
squeezed dry. For you I remember
bits of saints filling a vast room in Italy –
blackened ankle-bones, twisted finger-bones,
so-and-so's kneecap done forever with kneeling.
Around the body you once filled, others are pinned
in clusterings you never knew. At your shoulder
the tanager's scarlet is anemic; at your claws
the bunting's blue is faded and peppery.
This June morning, maybe, a descendent of yours
generations down the line
climbs and dips, moving gold, over a meadow.

6   to an osprey

Sometimes I get sick of shiny-paged bird books
with their close-ups both throwing me back in my chair and
pulling me forward, eager to savour such closeness,
all for a bird I've never seen.
                              High over the Public Gardens
you flap and coast and cry out, not much clear about you
but your voice and the bend of your wings.
Even as I say *you*, I know I'm talking to myself.

Today, no lovers on benches or babies in strollers,
as if wind had polished the pathways clean.
My neck strains back. You grow still vaguer, yet neither
the banked rhododendrons nor the pampered gardenias
hold my eye as you do, high above a fountain's mist
and frozen-in-stone goddesses and soldiers.

Sometimes I want that distance, a barely recognizable
                              pair of wings in the sky.

7   *to a brown-tailed shrike*

For a view of you, one sidetracked bird,
humans from afar – listers, twitchers, a clear-eyed crew –
burned up hundreds of miles and stood in the cold.

How did you end up in Bedford, Nova Scotia,
while your mate wintered in southeast Asia
gobbling newborn insects over a swamp?
Following months in a Russian forest, when did you
                                        take a wrong turn
away from the flock? Seas and latitudes later
strangers admired your black mask and rusty flanks,
scattered crickets and mealy worms
to lure you close –
                        but I wasn't there. So why speak
to you now? To murmur, "Sorry I didn't rush out
to catch a glimpse?" To beg, "Return next year, I'll
jump at the first chance"?
                                Meanwhile you wander
deeper into the rings of confusion, the only
brown-tailed shrike in North America,
doomed like an astronaut in a broken-off capsule.

You don't care a mealy worm you never met me.
I don't mind never having watched you –
or so it seems as the yard fills up with snow
wind-whipped so even the blue jays disappear.

8   to a sooty shearwater

You look like a chimney swift who can't find his way home
but this *is* your home. "Water, water everywhere" is your terra

firma, your eyes alighting on land less than ours
on water. Outside nesting season, only the wildest winds

drive you ashore. If your colour's dull, your flight's not:
a few quick wingbeats, then gliding low over everchanging waves

steady but shifting to the watery heaving, so close that it
sprinkles your feathers, or your wings slice it

in passing. What if some land bird always skimmed
that close to earth, ruffling grasses but never crashing

against rock or wood? Resting, you pick shrimp
from a crest, a trough. More quick beats – off

you glide again, wave-glancer, locomotion expert, quiet
but for a rare lamb-ish cry. For landlubbers at sea, *out there*

turns into *out here*, but our minds aren't big enough
to know your days as you know them, minute

to minute, flying through them, inches over breaking waves.

ACKNOWLEDGMENTS

Thanks to the editors of the following magazines and anthologies for giving several poems their first publications, often in earlier drafts:

The Antigonish Review: "Sloth Surprises," "Tree Trilogy"
Arc: "Diner in a Storm," "Three Windows"
Canadian Literature: "Under the Old Roof"
Event: "The Afterlife of Trees"
The Fiddlehead: "Listening on the Back Steps," "Lost Footnote for an Essay on Rhythm," "Talking to the Birds" (sections 1, 2, 7, 8, as sections 1, 2, 9, 10), "Two for the Winds"
Following the Plough, ed. John B. Lee (Black Moss Press, 2000): "A Toss of Cones"
Gaspereau Review: "How Acupuncture Is Like Poetry," "A Lake Named After My Ancestors"
Grain: "Talking to the Birds" (sections 4, 5, 6, as sections 5, 6, 8).
Landmarks: An Anthology of New Atlantic Canadian Poetry of the Land, ed. Hugh MacDonald and Brent MacLaine (The Acorn Press, 2001): "The Afterlife of Trees," "Under the Old Roof"
The Malahat Review: "Foot-doctor for the Homeless," "Hawthornden Improvisations" (1997 winner of the *Malahat Review* Long Poem Prize), "Sick for the New Millennium," "The Sonographer"
New Canadian Poetry, ed. Evan Jones (Fitzhenry and Whiteside, 2000): "The Afterlife of Trees," "A Toss of Cones"
Pottersfield Portfolio: "Graveyard Haiku"

Queen's Quarterly: "A Glosa for Joshua"

Writer's Forum: "Foot-doctor for the Homeless," first-prize
   winner in the 2000 Petra Kenney poetry awards, Lon-
   don, England. "Work at Twenty-One" received a 'high
   commendation' in the 1999 awards.

Special thanks to the members of a poetry workshop in
Halifax, and other friends, for invaluable editorial advice
during the writing of this book (1996–2001) and for the
pleasure of reading their poems. In particular, I'm grateful
to Sue MacLeod and Margo Wheaton for their suggestions
about the two long poems here. Also, much appreciation to
the Hawthornden Castle International Retreat for Writers;
to Don Coles and Alistair MacLeod for writing letters that
helped make the Scottish sojourn possible; and to Kerry
McSweeney of McGill-Queen's for keen fine-tuning help.
Belatedly, much gratitude to Derk Wynand, for longstand-
ing support.

Above all, to Karen, Joshua, and Laura, for being who they
are, and where they are.

Also by Brian Bartlett

Cattail Week
Planet Harbor
Underwater Carpentry
Granite Erratics